Adding Up THE Ads
KIDS AND ADVERTISING

By Tekla White

CONTENTS

Celebration Press
Pearson Learning Group

BUY! BUY! BUY!

Advertisements are everywhere. We see them on television, on the **Internet**, on posters in shop windows, and in magazines and newspapers. We hear them on our favorite radio program. Brand-name products shout from giant billboards and decorate our T-shirts.

Ads even arrive daily in the mail. In fact, the U.S. Postal Service delivers several million tons of junk, or unwanted, mail to Americans each year. The typical household in the United States receives more than 500 pieces of advertising mail yearly.

How many advertisements do you see and hear every day? Most likely it's in the hundreds. That's what some researchers estimate! The figure is higher if you spend a great deal of time listening to the radio or seeing ads on the streets of a large city.

Companies constantly advertise because they want you to buy their products. Most companies

Some products are almost exactly alike, even if their ads try to convince us that each one is the best.

have to sell many items to make a profit, and competition among them is fierce. They want to attract as many customers as possible.

In many cases there is very little difference in quality between competing brands. For example, most brands of toothpaste are much the same, so companies sponsor glitzy ad **campaigns** to make their product stand out. Many companies pay advertising agencies to make their ads. The ads try to persuade consumers that the company's product, not the competitor's, is the one to buy.

THE COST OF ADVERTISING

Advertising in the United States is BIG business. American companies spend more than $200 billion on advertising each year. In 1999 a well-known entertainment company spent $1.3 billion on ads, and a fast-food company spent $1.1 billion.

Companies buy time on television and space in magazines and newspapers. Ads cost more on TV shows that attract a very large audience. For example, a 30-second ad on the 2000 Super Bowl cost a staggering $2,100,000! On other programs the cost is less than half that amount.

Companies add the cost of advertising to the price of their products. Therefore, consumers—you and I—are the ones who really pay for the ads.

There are, however, some products that cost less because companies advertise. Publishing magazines and newspapers is expensive. Advertisers cover much of this cost when they pay to run ads in these publications. About one half of the space in a typical magazine is devoted to advertisements. Without the money from these ads, it would cost much more to buy our favorite magazines.

In the same way, commercials help pay the cost of broadcasting television and radio shows. The programs that corporations agree to sponsor are the ones that find slots in the program lineup. These are shows that the advertisers believe will attract an audience that is likely to buy their products. If no company wants to buy ads during your favorite television show, then the show won't last long!

◀ The things we buy often cost extra because companies have to pay for advertising.

Many American young people have a
lot of money to spend however they like.

HOW COMPANiES TARGET THEiR ADS

Successful companies determine who their best customers are—often by age, sex, job, hobbies, income, or where they live. Then they design ads to appeal to certain groups.

Many companies target young people. Researchers estimate that 6- to 11-year-olds in the United States have about $17 million a year in spending money. They tend to buy name-brand products for clothing and toys. In addition, they influence their parents to buy items costing about $150 billion a year—from their favorite car to household goods.

TECHNiQUES ADVERTiSERS USE

Advertisers use a variety of ways to persuade people to use a product or service. Most begin with a basic **appeal**, or message. It explains the product and gives reasons for using it. Advertisers also use special persuasive techniques—often several in the same ad.

These techniques may prevent you from thinking clearly. If you are aware of these techniques, however, you will be able to make better decisions. Ask yourself what the product will do for you. Examine the evidence. The most commonly used special techniques are discussed below.

Advertising Language Many ads contain special—and often misleading—language. Advertisers are not allowed to make false claims about products, but they can make the products seem appealing by playing with words. The words *awesome*, *fabulous*, and *great* sound impressive. But they don't give any useful information about the product.

Examine the ads when such words are used. Because they offer opinions, not facts, these words simply tell you that the maker of the product thinks it is great, awesome, or fabulous. You'll notice that the ads seldom say why the shampoo or peanut butter is great or what it can do for you.

It's easy to be influenced by advertising language. However, you can train yourself to watch for special or "**loaded**" **words** that often appear in ads.

The word *help* is frequently used. Products "*help* stop coughs fast" or "*help* take out spots." The ads don't claim that the product actually does the job!

Comparing Some ads compare their product to another brand's product. Sometimes they compare them directly and name the other product or call it Brand X. For example, a yogurt company might promise that its special yogurt is richer and creamier than more expensive brands.

Other times the ads don't really compare their product to anything. An ad might claim that its cereal is *better*. But what is it *better* than?

Advertisements often compare a product to other brands.

Appeal to Emotions Many advertisers create ads that appeal to the emotions, not to common sense. Some ads play on people's fears. Others appeal to their desire for beauty or success. Ads for some products suggest they will make the user attractive. For example, an ad may suggest that wearing a certain brand of makeup will make the user the center of attention at a party.

"Hurry-Up" Ads Advertisers also use special ads to get customers to buy quickly, before they realize that they don't really need the product. Advertisers may tell people that an offer is good only for a *"limited time."* Or they advertise a specific product at a low price *"while supplies last."* When you see such ads, stop and think and ask yourself: Do I really need this product NOW?

Selling Lifestyles These advertisements show popular, happy, glamorous, or successful people using a particular product. The words and images of the ads suggest that using the brand will make customers just as glamorous or happy as the models in the ads. People who are unhappy or believe they are unpopular may respond to such ads.

Bandwagon Appeal A bandwagon carries a band in a parade. "To climb on the bandwagon" is to join a winning group.

Bandwagon-appeal ads suggest that everyone else is buying a product and if you're not, you are a big loser! The purpose is to persuade customers to do what everyone else is doing. Such ads claim their brands are "the best sellers" or "the most popular" or the ones "all the kids are buying."

Some advertisers play on young people's fear of being left out if they don't have certain products. In such ads, the young person with the advertised computer game, sports equipment, or lunch item is smiling and surrounded by friends.

Bandwagon-appeal ads try to persuade people to buy a product so that they will be part of the winning group.

I wish my parents
had bought a
Super Homework Helper
computer program!

Have you ever noticed what happens in an ad when parents serve the "best-selling" brand of snack or other food? The whole family—and sometimes the whole neighborhood—crowds into the kitchen. The parents are so popular!

Of course, we know that these things happen only in ads. Resist jumping on the bandwagon and buying a product just because others are doing it.

Faulty Cause and Effect Ads Some ads claim, without proof, that certain good results will come from the use of their products. Consider breakfast cereals, for example. There are so many competing brands—each trying to find a way to stand out among the others. Cereals now come in all sizes, colors, and shapes. Some are filled with vitamins, promising better health. Others promise to be delicious. Some even promise to be fun. Think about what the product can actually deliver.

Even household appliance ads sometimes promise happiness. An ad for a vacuum cleaner

shows a family enjoying a day at an amusement park. It suggests they have time for fun because they have that speedy vacuum! The advertiser may even throw in a coupon for the park, hoping that children will talk their parents into buying the vacuum.

Testimonial Ads

Testimonials are statements that support products. Such ads feature experts, famous people, or just ordinary people. Companies spend billions of dollars on testimonial ads each year.

Why might a testimonial from a well-known person such as Tiger Woods influence people to buy a product?

Popular athletes may earn millions of dollars when they **endorse**, or support, products. Often they earn more for making advertisements than they do for playing their sport! They try to convince the public that they must wear the same kind of shoes, drink the same brand of beverage, or use the same kind of sports equipment as the athletes do to be winners.

Because some people choose to imitate sports heroes whom they wish to be like, such advertisements can cause great demand for a product. A shortage of high-priced, trendy sneakers that were endorsed by a famous basketball star once nearly caused a riot at a Sacramento, California, mall. A shoe store ran out of the limited number of the new type of sneakers they had for sale. Young people had camped out all night in front of the store to buy the shoes and were extremely disappointed and irritated. Other shoe stores across the United States experienced scuffles and unrest among customers because of shortages, too.

Remember that celebrities are acting when they appear in commercials. ▶

In addition to famous athletes, movie and television stars also earn millions of dollars endorsing products. Some people think the brand of shampoo an actor endorses must be the best one. After all, she is a big star. Others just find the actor appealing, which colors their feelings about the product.

Remember that stars earn money for acting in advertisements just as they do for other acting work. Notice that stars don't always say they actually use the product. Just holding the product in the ad makes people think they do.

Some doctors and dentists share in the advertising dollars by endorsing health products or services. These experts are paid well for their appearances in ads. They may not really be there to talk about people's health, but rather to persuade people to buy a product or service. Some "experts" are just actors playing a part.

When dentists in ads say they recommend a brand of mouthwash to their patients, it sounds as if they believe it's the best brand to buy. But what do the ads really say? The dentists recommend the mouthwash, but they may also think other brands are just as good. They just don't say so.

Product Characters Sometimes companies pay to use well-known cartoon or fictional characters on their products. Advertisers feel sure that customers will buy the shampoo featuring the character rather than the shampoo in a plain bottle, even though the two products are similar.

Companies pitch their product character ads to young people because the characters appeal to so many children. Advertisers believe that children

Many kids will want this shampoo simply because their favorite cartoon character, Zerbo, is featured in the ad.

Zerbo's Mission:

to make shampooing fun!

will think of the brand with the character and want to buy the product.

Other Techniques Though an old technique, **repetition** still works. Companies run their ads often on TV and radio and in newspapers and magazines.

Slogans are short phrases that are catchy and easily remembered. Used over and over, slogans create a favorable image of a product. **Humor** is also a very important technique. People like to laugh, and they remember funny ads.

17

ADVERTiSiNG iN UNEXPECTED PLACES

Companies sometimes advertise in ways you may not even be aware of. You meet advertising in movies, on the Internet, in schools, in magazine **advertorials** and TV **infomercials**, and on clothing and other items.

At the Movies If you go to the movies to escape from TV ads, you'll often see that the advertisers got there first. The **logos** on actors' sneakers, the brands on the clothes they wear, and the sodas they drink are seen right along with the movie stars. Advertisers pay from about $10,000 to $1,000,000 just for their product to be shown for a few seconds in a big film. The same type of advertising also appears on your favorite TV shows.

On the Internet Many companies also sponsor Internet Web sites. Kids can go to the sites and play games with their favorite brand-name characters.

The games you play on Internet Web sites sometimes turn out to be advertisements in disguise!

Ads are even mixed in with the puzzles kids work and the games they play on the Web. Ads that look like part of the game can pop up while they're playing. Then players must often plow through long ads called roadblocks just to finish a game.

Web games are very popular. They are played by thousands of kids every day. Those who play often register their e-mail address, age, and special interests. This information gives advertisers a target group of possible customers for their products.

In Schools You may get ready, get set, and make a run for school to avoid ads. But you won't get away with it. Students see advertising even in school.

Commercials are part of some classroom TV news programs. The programs are beamed to the schools for free, but watching the advertisements is part of the deal. Some parents have objected to the presence of ads in the classroom news.

Maybe there's no television in your classroom. But take a look at your classroom current-events magazines. Many of these publications feature advertisements as well as information about the world.

There's even more. Some free educational materials display company logos, or trademarks, and ads. Many free nutrition charts come to classrooms with free food samples, in case you'd like to buy more.

Sometimes advertisers plaster free pencils and book covers with ads and logos. If you watch your team play football, you may see an ad for a soft drink on the scoreboard. Companies pay millions of advertising dollars to reach you at school and believe it to be a good investment.

In Advertorials When you read your favorite magazine, ads might not seem to be a big deal. You know where they are, so you can just skip over them if you wish. But be on the lookout for advertorials.

Always read the fine print above an article. You may find that your magazine has ads that look like regular articles.

Advertorials are advertisements that look just like information articles or editorials. For example, fashion or food advertising can be disguised as an advice column that tells you what to buy to solve a problem or how to have the best party ever.

Some advertisers try to match the look of the magazine's editorial pages. They want the advertorials to appear to be just ordinary articles. The word *advertisement* appears in tiny type at the top of the first page.

In Infomercials Some television channels show half-hour or even hour-long programs that tell viewers about great new products, fabulous deals, or amazing health breakthroughs. These programs feature items such as exercise machines, kitchenware, and jewelry. Often a celebrity or "expert" talks about the benefits of the product. Of course, these programs are really just extra-long commercials, which are called infomercials.

In Other Places Sometimes people advertise products without even knowing it. They carry large umbrellas and shopping bags displaying advertisers' names. Their jeans and backpacks may display company logos or characters from movies and popular books. They wear jackets and caps supporting sports teams or advertising products.

If you wear a certain best-selling brand, it can make you feel like one of the in-group. But name-brand products cost a lot more than plain items without the logos. What do you think? Are they worth the extra money?

Do you want to be a walking advertisement for special products?

BE A SMART CONSUMER

We are surrounded with advertisements for products and services, and many of those products and services are excellent. However it's smart to base choices on product quality rather than on ad appeal. Before you break open your piggy bank to buy the latest fad, check out these tips for cool consumers.

✔ Think before you buy. Do you really need this item? Is this product or service better than one that costs less?
✔ Keep in mind that celebrities who advertise a product are paid for their work. It's a job!
✔ Remember that cartoon characters don't make products better. They just make them cost more.
✔ Take your time and try to compare products.
✔ Think critically about ads. What do the words in the ads really mean?